A Mother

is a

Gift

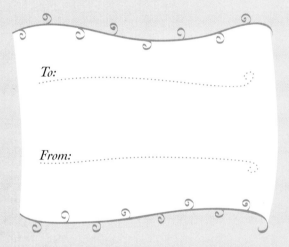

To: ⋯⋯⋯⋯⋯⋯⋯⋯⋯⋯⋯⋯⋯⋯⋯⋯⋯

From: ⋯⋯⋯⋯⋯⋯⋯⋯⋯⋯⋯⋯⋯⋯⋯⋯

A Mother is a Gift

Illustrated by Alexis Siroc

WARNER BOOKS

An AOL Time Warner Company

Copyright © 2003 by Redbridge LLC
Illustrations copyright © 2003 by Spinning Plates Studio

Warner Book, Inc., 1271 Avenue of the Americas, New York, NY 10020

Visit our Web site at www.twbookmark.com.

Printed in the United States of America

First Printing: April 2003

10   9   8   7   6   5   4   3   2   1

Library of Congress Cataloging-in-Publication Data

A mother is a gift.

    p.cm.

  ISBN 0-446-53114-6

    1. Mothers. 2. Gift books. I. Warner Books (Firm)

HQ759 M87313 2003

306.874'3--dc21

                              2002033152

Design by Alexis Siroc

God couldn't be everywhere.
That's why mothers exist!

A Mother
is a Gift

"Whatever else is unsure…

a mother's love is not."

—JAMES JOYCE

When Michelangelo unveiled his *Pietà* in 1499, not every critic was pleased with his sculpture of Mary cradling her lifeless son. Some complained that the figure of Mary was "too large." Pondering the comment, Michelangelo replied, "I disagree. For surely a mother must have a generous lap."

A mother's lap needs to be ample. That's something every schoolchild knows. Soft and warm, cozy and welcoming, a lap is a place to curl up for a nap, listen to a story, or go to for a tender snuggle. Whether covered by an apron, cradling a ball of yarn, or holding a book, a mama's lap is a place of comforts. It's where many of us first grasped one of life's eternal verities: that a mother is a gift.

Mother. Take a minute, if you will, and meditate on the word. Let it filter through your mind and sink into your consciousness. If the experience unleashes a flood tide of memories, don't be surprised. From the time Eve gave birth to the world's first children, motherhood has been a complicated role. Sizing it up can be daunting.

Soft and warm, cozy and welcoming

For many of us, the word *mother* transports us back to our childhood, when we were small and incapable of fending for ourselves. Ever present and all powerful, mother was the force at the center of our universe who gave us life and helped sustain it. If we wailed for food, mama gave us milk. If we yearned for sleep, she rocked us in her arms. Like a steadfast soldier standing watch by our bedside, mother was the sentinel who banished the bogeyman, taught us our prayers, and ushered in good dreams.

As we grew up and ventured out into the world, mother's role expanded. Like an enchanted shape shifter changing parts on cue, she not only helped with home-

work and sorted out our Halloween costumes, she also mended our broken hearts and forgave us our trespasses. Serving as healer, troubleshooter, nurturer, and confessor, mother was our jack-of-all-trades in the school of hard knocks. When the lesson plan got rough and we were at risk of failing, she was the nurse on call who provided first aid.

How she did it was simple. She did it with love, a pure and inexhaustible supply. So great and unconditional was this love that it enabled her to move mountains that got in her way. Depending on what was required, she could be sacrificing, selfless, and compassionate—or as ferocious and combative as a mother lioness defending her cubs.

"Whatever else is unsure in this stinking dunghill o' a world," the novelist James Joyce once wrote, "a mother's love is not." Joyce was merely acknowledging what is evident to all who can see: that a mother is a gift.

The Gifts a Mother Brings

"Some are kissing mothers and some are scolding mothers, but it is love just the same."

—PEARL S. BUCK

*I*magine you've been asked to oversee a new organization—let's call it the Mothers Hall of Fame. Lots of candidates want to be inducted into this club, but it's up to you to determine who gets elected. Bestowing the honors, you soon realize, can be a tricky proposition. Your first hurdle is answering the question: What are the qualities that make a mother outstanding?

Ask a dozen people what constitutes an ideal mother and you're bound to get a dozen answers. A mother seen as "attentive" through one set of eyes might be viewed as "intrusive" through another, while an "exceptionally loving" mother sometimes comes across as "smothering." What makes a good mother, it seems, is for each in turn to decide.

Even so, there are some qualities of mothering that everybody takes for granted. For instance, most people expect a good mother to keep her little ones

Flowing from a perfect and unbreakable heart of caring

clean, well fed, and protected. Ensuring there's food in the cupboard and clean socks in the bottom drawer is one of a mother's basic responsibilities.

But being an *outstanding* mother involves more. Great mothers, by nature, coddle their children in a thick blanket of warmth and affection. Creating an atmosphere of tenderness and safekeeping involves a generosity of spirit that helps a mother elevate the needs of her offspring above her own.

As one adult child recently described it, "My mother was born with a master's degree in sacrifice. If there wasn't enough baked ziti when we were eating Sunday dinner, she'd pass the pan and say she was on

Weight Watchers. Given the choice to take or give, there was no question what mother would do."

The rare and precious gift of unconditional love is at the heart of such actions. So special is this brand of affection that it motivates a mother to dip into her deep well of generosity while assuring children they need not "be good" or "behave"—or be anything—to be loved. Flowing from a perfect and unbreakable heart of caring, such love is available in infinite supply, always and forever!

Yet the greatness of a mother's unconditional love doesn't preclude discipline. Caring mothers don't raise spoiled children who think they rule the roost.

Grasping the importance of community and inter-dependence, good mothers try to instill a sense of social responsibility and moral character in their offspring, combining the "be your own person" mindset with a "share your toys" philosophy.

"Good mothers draw lines in the sand," one kindergarten teacher recently noted. "They may think that the sun rises and sets on their child, but their unspoken goal is to prevent the little one from being swept away by an undertow of selfishness."

As anyone who has paid attention knows, a mother's way of disciplining is special. Moving with mercurial speed between kissing and scolding, a wise mother avoids holding grudges; she weighs her child's actions in the light of the intentions that produced them and never lets the sun set on an argument. As the novelist Pearl Buck so aptly put it, "Some are kissing mothers and some are scolding mothers, but it is love just the same, and most mothers kiss and scold together."

Perhaps at the root of this masterful balancing act is the "maternal instinct." Call it a sixth sense, every good mother uses this ability to shine a searchlight inside her children to see what's happening there. As one adult child recently put it, "My mother knows what's going on with me before there's a shred of information. Out of the blue she'll call and ask, 'What's wrong?'"

A mother's intuition may explain how a mom can hear what a child does not say, or know when it's time to come off the sideline and intervene in her children's lives. Fathers routinely marvel at a mother's knack for precision timing. "Whether she is overseeing our five-year-old son as he struggles to tie his own sneakers, or watching our frustrated twenty-year-old daughter break up with her boyfriend," one admiring husband explained, "my wife knows when to get involved. That's one reason she's the 'go-to' authority in our children's lives."

Dad is right. Although some say that the father is the head of the household, the mother is often "the neck that turns the head." Whenever trouble is brewing, the children know to holler for mama. And so does dad! His frequently uttered phrase—"Ask your mother"—acknowledges mom's role as chief judge with the deciding vote in the family's court.

But let's leave court for the moment and return to the Mothers Hall of Fame. In our quest to determine what defines an outstanding mother, we've illuminated devotion, love, intuition, and caring as important qualities. Mothers kiss and scold and never let the sun go down on their anger. Surely these virtues are some of the hallmarks distinguishing great mothers.

But maybe greatness boils down to one characteristic that ties all the virtues together. When all is said and done, motherhood may simply be the act of *leading* children in the hope of *serving* their best interests. Or to put it another way, motherhood is a rare and inspired form of *"servant leadership."* Realizing it's better to be a model rather than a critic, good mothers lead by example, understanding that children are inspired to embrace new ideas by seeing them embodied in someone they admire.

The great poet Emerson once observed that "No child will accomplish anything excellent or commanding except when they listen to the whisper which is heard by them alone." At heart, that is every mother's fervent wish: to raise an independent, confident, and self-assured child who has the vision and the fortitude to strive to reach their dreams as they proceed along the road of life. But even before that occurs, children must first hear the whisper of the voice within that tells the simple truth: that a mother is a gift.

The Gift of
Holding on Tight

"Not yet. Please don't go!"

—A CHILD STARTING SCHOOL

Oh, it's you. Come closer. Take a peak at this familiar scene. It's early morning on the first day of school and little children everywhere are putting on their squeaky new sneakers and colorful backpacks as they prepare to embark on the journey of a lifetime. In bustling cities on drizzly mornings, in rural towns on sunny roads, and in suburban centers under cloudy skies, the little boys and girls are setting off to begin their new life as students. Today, for the very first time, many will leave the warm nest in which their mama nurtured them and begin the solo flight.

Look! Some are arriving at the school yard just across the way. Plagued by butterflies in the stomach and a severe outbreak of first-grade jitters, they're gathering in little clusters of twos and threes, hoping they won't run up against a "bully" or get assigned to 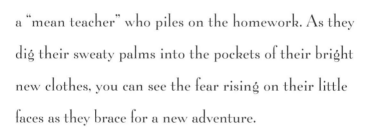 a "mean teacher" who piles on the homework. As they dig their sweaty palms into the pockets of their bright new clothes, you can see the fear rising on their little faces as they brace for a new adventure.

Oh, no. The hands of the clock are approaching nine A.M.! That's when the school bells will clang, summoning everyone to class. Like panic-stricken sailors heading into a nor'easter, the little newcomers begin

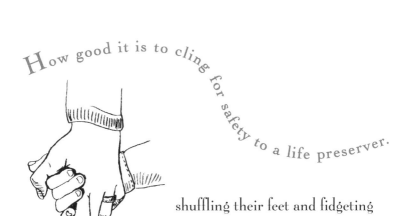

How good it is to cling for safety to a life preserver.

shuffling their feet and fidgeting
nervously. If the thoughts echoing in
their heads were audible, we'd probably hear the sound
of this script being recited over and over:

Not yet. Please don't go!

Just one more minute.

Instinctively, they tighten their grip on the hand
of the one who brought them. For, you see, they are not
alone. Their mothers are with them, right by their

sides, just where you would expect them to be on such a momentous occasion. And when you think about it, how could they be soothed any other way?

Mama! Mama! some of the little ones cry out. Inching closer to the pilot who has gotten them through every storm they have weathered in life is a reaction as natural as the nervous pounding of the little hearts beating in their chests. Locking eyes with mama helps steady their wave-tossed boats against the rising tide of fear. Has she ever once failed to calm the churning in their stomachs? Will this change now?

Just one more minute, she reassures, squeezing their hand. Drawing near to their understanding mother, the children breathe a sigh of relief. How good it is to cling for safety to a life preserver. And a mother's hand is certainly that. For as young and innocent as they may be, these pint-sized people have already mastered one of life's most profound truths: that a mother's hand is a precious gift.

The Gift of
Mommy Talk

"Remember to say
'Please' and 'Thank you.'"

—MOTHERS EVERYWHERE

*H*ave you ever heard of a "mommily"? About twenty-five years ago the term was coined to describe the special manner of speaking associated with mothers. *Just wait until your father gets home* was a quintessential mommily back then, but there were hundreds of other pearls of wisdom in the mommily dictionary. Popular favorites included: *Because I said so. Be home before dark. Remember to say please and thank you.* And the all-time classic: *Wear clean underwear—you never know when you might get into an accident.*

It cannot be denied that mothers have a special way of talking. Combining gentle imperatives, sugar-coated orders, and veiled threats, the language of mothers is lovingly dictatorial. Spanning all cultures and backgrounds, "motherspeak" is designed to instruct, reprimand, and convey affection all at once and with ruthless honesty. Just like our mothers themselves!

What is it that creates the signature style of mothers? Mincing no words, they make it their mission to speak with candor whenever the mood strikes them. "If my lipstick is too dark or my slip is showing or the speech I gave was too long," one daughter said recently, "I can count on my mother to tell me."

Whether by right or by privilege, mothers feel entitled to make their feelings and opinions known.

Because I said so.

Remember to say please and thank you.

Be home before dark.

Just wait until your father gets home.

And when it comes right down to it, why not? After all, who carried us in the womb for nine months and gave us life? Who sang us our first lullabies, nursed us at the breast, and was a constant companion in our endlessly monotonous diaper days? Who potty-trained us, wiped our runny noses, and treated our chicken pox? If you're a mother, you know the answer. If you *have* a mother, you know the answer. The answer is, your mother.

Long before they began sprouting mommilies, most mothers were practicing what the poet Elizabeth Barrett Browning called the art of "kissing full sense into empty words." Exchanging "goo-goo" and "ga-ga"

in tireless sessions of baby talk may have prepared a mother for the day she reminds us to "wear clean underwear." Though the advice may seem silly, it's really precious when you remember that our mothers once patted our wet bottoms dry and powdered them too!

Shh! Though it isn't polite to eavesdrop, let's listen in as a mother talks to her child . . .

When you get there, call me. . . . And remember your manners. . . . Why? . . . Because I said so. . . .

Sound familiar?

The Gift of *Influence*

"All I am, I owe to my mother."

—George Washington

When Mrs. Williamson volunteered to participate in her community's safety patrol, an administrator asked her if she was "a mother" or if she "worked." "I was astonished by the question," she later remembered. "As if the two are opposites."

Of course they aren't. At least not in the minds of most sensible people. In the not too distant past, however, there was a widespread presumption that because mothers didn't earn a paycheck, they weren't working. Since child rearing was an unpaid role performed mostly by women, it was not especially valued.

Times have changed, but there's still a long way to go. Still muddying the waters is the term "working mother," which was coined when women began juggling children and careers outside the home. As the columnist Liz Smith notes, the term "working mother" implies "that any mother without a definite career is indolently not working, lolling around eating bonbons, reading novels, and watching soap operas."

Let's set the record straight once and for all. Being a mother is one of the most important and backbreaking jobs in the world. Since the beginning of time, mothers have not only brought new life into the world, carrying it in the womb and delivering it through hard labor, they've reared the world's children and shaped the character of individuals and nations. The French emperor Napoleon acknowledged as much when he said, "Let France have good mothers and she will have good sons." And who can forget the famous words of William Ross Wallace, who wrote in 1865 that "The hand that rocks the cradle is the hand that rules the world."

When a mother gives birth, she holds eternity in her arms, safeguards the promise of the future, and influences everything it holds. In the cradle she rocks may be a son who will grow up to be a peacemaker who settles wars and reunites torn nations. The little girl she nurses to sleep at night may one day become a senator who writes legislation to help feed the world's starving children and to help house its homeless. Her

...they've reared the world's children and

Today's Lesson

shaped the character of individuals and nations...

41

son might be a president who brings democratic ideals to a new nation because he has learned justice, fairness, and truth at the knee of a woman who understands the merits of compassion, gentleness, and kindness— his mother.

Toward the end of his life, George Washington so eloquently said, "All I am I owe to my mother. I attribute all my success in life to the moral, intellectual, and physical education I received from her."

So, to the question are you a mother or do you work: Let the answer be a resounding "Yes."

The Gift of a
Shoulder
to Cry On

"A mother is not a person to lean on but a person to make leaning unnecessary."

—CANFIELD FISHER

When you were very little, did you ever experience a "no-good very-bad day"? This was the kind of day when there seemed to be no end in sight to the downward spiral of awful happenings. You lost your homework *and* didn't get a part in the school play. The teacher gave a surprise quiz and you missed scoring the winning basket in the season final. All you wanted to do was crawl under a rock and never come out. But you couldn't find a rock big enough. Instead, you went home to the one person who could make you forget that any of it ever happened. That person, of course, was your mother.

When the chips are down, mothers have a way of coming through. They do it not necessarily by offering solutions—sometimes our mothers do nothing but serve as witnesses to our sorrow. Nor do they help by saying anything special. The comfort they provide comes from standing by, quietly listening, as we pour out our hearts. A mother's special power is the ability to be there with a *desire to help,* any time, any where. A shoulder to cry on whenever we come knocking is a mother's special gift.

That said, leaning on our mothers is complicated. Though we seek their help in times of difficulty, many children go through life struggling to gain independence from their mother's powerful influence. "Attract/repel may best describe how I relate to my mother," one son said, speaking in candor. "I love her without reservation. But to be my own person has sometimes meant bucking her authority to show her that I'm my own person."

Seeing how far the umbilical cord can stretch without breaking is part of the drama of growing up. Children yank the cord and mothers tug back. The children yank again and she tries to reel them in. Getting to the point where our mothers acknowledge that we are "our own person" is a journey that leads from separation anxiety to separate identities. It takes time and can involve plenty of struggle. Maybe it begins for most children on the first day of school, when the bell rings and mom heads for the exit, leaving them alone and unprotected. Though frightened and per-plexed, they're strangely exhilarated being out there on the ledge by themselves.

"Billy likes to test me," one mom said of her five-year-old son. "I understand what's going on. He's just a little bird spreading his wings, getting ready to take flight."

While still in the nest, however, several truths must be acknowledged about fledglings. First of all, in this vast universe full of billions of mothers, each little peeper gets just one mama to watch over him. What extraordinary destiny has placed us in the life we have with our particular mother. Our relationship with her is singular and deserving of immense respect. We belong to our mother alone and she to us.

Second, to most of the world, our mothers are average. Though in our minds we make them out to be

The keeper of the flame in the heart

saints and saviors, heroes and villains, most of them are people who will never win a beauty pageant or the Pulitzer prize or an Olympic gold medal. You are never going to read about them in the newspapers or see them on television. Most live quiet, unassuming lives that get celebrated once a year when Mother's Day rolls around. They have faults and failings as do we. And we must never hold our mothers to a higher standard than that to which we hold ourselves.

And finally, our mothers may not always have the best advice or the solution to our problems, but most possess a caring heart. They want to be there for us when we need them. A man once said that the most important thing a child can know is that someone is waiting on the other side of the door, listening for their footsteps when they get home. To be expected by someone is one of the best feelings in the world. To be expected by our mother is best of all. For she is the one who keeps the fire burning for us, the keeper of the flame in the heart—our mother.

The Gift of the Magic Mirror

"Mother knows best."

—EDNA FERBER

When Olivia was eighteen years old, she found a book titled *How Not to Be Like Your Mother* sitting in a bookstore beside another volume called *My Mother, My Self.* "Do you think we are like our mother?" Olivia asked her sixteen-year-old sister, Gemma. "Do we want to be?"

The journey toward discovering our true identity leads many of us to examine the influence of the many people who raised us. A single lifetime may not be long enough to figure out all the impressions made by our relatives and friends. But as sure as eye color and hair texture have been passed down through biology, our mothers have influenced our beings and who we are today.

"I inherited a cheerful disposition from my mother," a woman named Barbara said recently. "Her people skills and outgoing nature seemed to have rubbed off." Michael, on the other hand, says he is moody and impatient, quick to anger and pessimistic. "When I exhibit these traits," he confesses, "people say, 'Just like your mother.'"

For better or worse, we are who we are. With time and effort, some of our character traits can be modified. But, more important, there's a question every son and daughter must answer. Will they resent what has been

53

inherited, as the British novelist Somerset Maugham seemed to be doing when he wrote that "Few misfortunes can befall a boy which bring worse conse- quences than to have a really affectionate mother"?

Or will we live in the spirit of gratitude reflected by Celine Dion in her song "Because of You"? Dedicated to her mother, the lyrics suggest that the singer believes she owes all of her success to her mother.

When we look into the magic mirror of self-reflection held in front of us by our mother, we have a choice to make. We can value what we've inherited—or disown it. Either way, it cannot be denied that a mother gives the gift of self-discovery, leading us to insights as we undertake our life's journey.

My Mother,
My Gift:
What I Love Most
about My Mother

*E*very mother is special because every mother is different. What is unique about yours? On the following pages some space has been provided for you to jot down your special recollections about your mother.

"In search of my mother's garden,

I found my own.

—ALICE WALKER

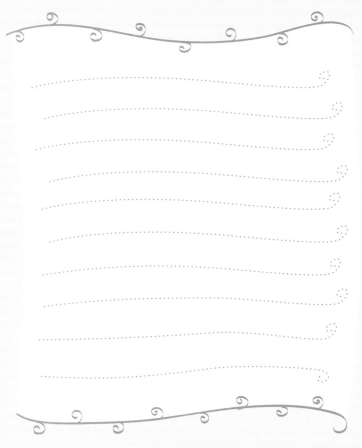

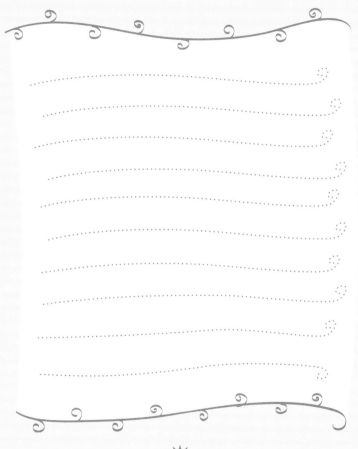

Personal Observations about

Mothers and Motherhood

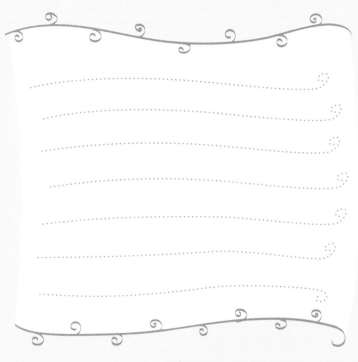

Resources

Use of the following books is gratefully acknowledged in the research and compilation of this book:

A Book of Love for My Son,
by H. Jackson Brown, Jr. and Hy Brett

A Book of Love for My Daughter,
by H. Jackson Brown, Jr., Paula Y. Flautt, and Kim Shea

A World of Ideas, by Chris Rohmann

Bartlett's Book of Familiar Quotations, 16th edition

Bartlett's Book of Anecdotes, Revised edition

The Complete Book of Bible Quotations from the New Testament, edited by Mark L. Levine and Eugene Rachlis

The Complete Book of Bible Quotations from the Old Testament, edited by Mark L. Levine and Eugene Rachlis

The Fabric of Friendship

Quotationary, by Leonard Roy Frank